SAVE OUR EARTH!
Climate Action Explained

REDUCING AIR POLLUTION

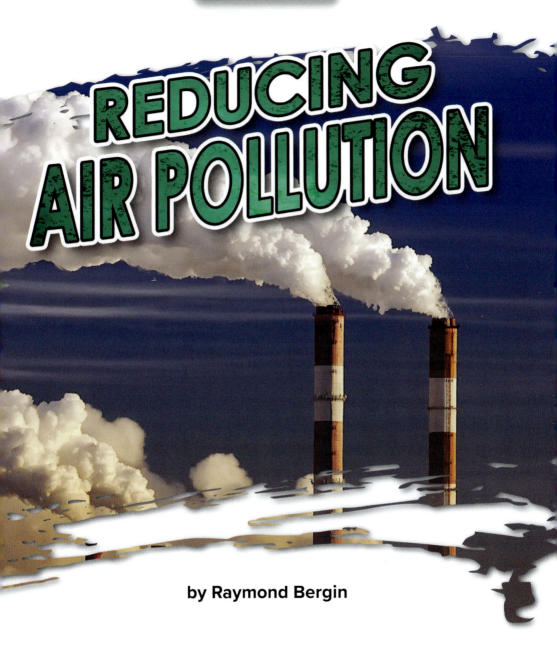

by Raymond Bergin

Minneapolis, Minnesota

Credits
Cover and title page, © as_trofey/Adobe Stock ; 4–5, © Kevin Izorce/Alamy Stock Photo; 6–7, © buradaki/Shutterstock; 8–9, © Sandip Neogi/Shutterstock; 10–11, © Tribune Content Agency LLC/Alamy Stock Photo; 12, © Mark Smith/Shutterstock; 12–13, © giovannicaito/iStock; 14–15, © Trevor Bexon/Shutterstock; 16–17, © Florian Kopp/Alamy Stock Photo; 19, © Bloomberg/Getty Images; 20–21, © Bloomberg/Getty Images; 22–23, © Simon Maina/Getty Images; 25, © Mukuru Clean Stoves; 26–27, © Holli/Shutterstock; 28, © bernardbodo/iStock; 29TL, © FatCamera/iStock; 29UML, © Africa Studio/Adobe Stock; 29ML, © ink drop/Adobe Stock; 29BML, © Alexey Rotanov/Adobe Stock; 29BL, © LeoPatrizi/iStock

Bearport Publishing Company Product Development Team
Publisher: Jen Jenson; Director of Product Development: Spencer Brinker; Managing Editor: Allison Juda; Editor: Cole Nelson; Associate Editor: Tiana Tran; Production Editor: Naomi Reich; Designer: Kim Jones; Designer: Kayla Eggert; Designer: Steve Scheluchin; Production Specialist: Owen Hamlin

Statement on Usage of Generative Artificial Intelligence
Bearport Publishing remains committed to publishing high-quality nonfiction books. Therefore, we restrict the use of generative AI to ensure accuracy of all text and visual components pertaining to a book's subject. See BearportPublishing.com for details.

Library of Congress Cataloging-in-Publication Data is available at www.loc.gov or upon request from the publisher.

ISBN: 979-8-89577-049-8 (hardcover)
ISBN: 979-8-89577-166-2 (ebook)

Copyright © 2026 Bearport Publishing Company. All rights reserved. No part of this publication may be reproduced in whole or in part, stored in any retrieval system, or transmitted in any form or by any means, electronic, mechanical, photocopying, recording, or otherwise, without written permission from the publisher. Bearport Publishing is a division of FlutterBee Education Group.

For more information, write to Bearport Publishing, 3500 American Blvd W, Suite 150, Bloomington, MN 55431.

Contents

Something in the Air 4
Earth's Security Blanket 6
Filthy Fuel 8
Air Quality Alert! 10
Poisonous Progress 12
Up in Smoke 14
Home Is Where the Harm Is 16
Fertile Fields: Takachar 18
Battery Power: Ampd Energy 20
Green Machines: Roam 22
Clean Cooking: Mukuru Clean Stove 24
Breathing Easier 26

Reduce Air Pollution! 28
Glossary 30
Read More 31
Learn More Online 31
Index 32
About the Author 32

Something in the Air

Traffic clogs the streets of the city, and **exhaust** streams out of every tailpipe. Huge plumes of smoke belch out from a nearby factory, too, hiding the skyline behind a cloud of **smog**. A forest outside the city has been on fire for days, and wind brings wildfire smoke into people's homes. There, it mixes with chemicals poisoning the air from cleaning products and wall paint. The air all around is full of pollution. What on Earth is going on here, and how can we fix it?

Globally, about 8.1 million people die annually due to air pollution. On average, air pollution shortens people's lives by 2.3 years.

Earth's Security Blanket

All that separates Earth from space is a layer of gases called the **atmosphere**. This structure is often described as a protective bubble or blanket around the planet. It contains gases that all life on Earth needs, such as **oxygen** that animals breathe and **carbon dioxide** that plants use to turn sunlight into energy.

Earth's atmosphere is made up of mostly nitrogen. In addition, there is oxygen as well as small amounts of carbon dioxide, methane, water vapor, and other gases.

Some of the gases in the atmosphere trap the sun's heat around the planet, much like the glass walls of a greenhouse. These so-called greenhouse gases make Earth warm enough to support life.

Without the atmosphere, days would be blazing hot and nights would be icy cold. The planet's average temperature would be about −0.4 degrees Fahrenheit (−18°C).

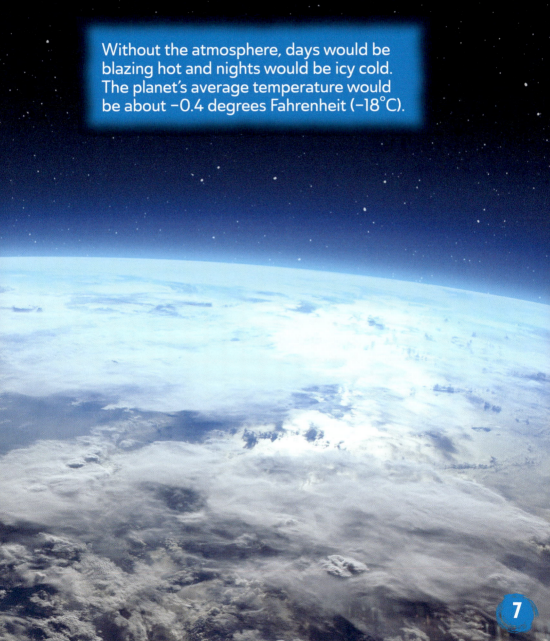

Filthy Fuel

Human actions are upsetting the balance of gases in the atmosphere. Much of the energy needed to keep our world running comes from **fossil fuels**. When these fuels are burned, they release pollutants into the air.

One of the most harmful pollutants is the greenhouse gas carbon dioxide. This gas is naturally found in the atmosphere. However, the extra carbon dioxide from burning fossil fuels is trapping more heat around the planet. This is making Earth's temperatures rise and is changing the weather around the world.

Every year, human activity produces more than 35 billion tons (32 billion t) of carbon dioxide. Once released, this gas can stay in the atmosphere for hundreds or thousands of years!

Air Quality Alert!

Beyond heating Earth, air pollution also poisons our planet. Transportation is a major contributor to these harmful **emissions**. Fuel-burning vehicles release carbon monoxide, nitrogen oxide, and ammonia.

These gases cause smog that poisons the air plants and animals take in. Harmful emissions from transportation also create **acid rain** that adds pollutants to the water and soil. The emissions can even strip oxygen out of smaller bodies of water, such as lakes and ponds, creating dead zones where nothing can live.

> Air pollution is everywhere. The World Health Organization estimates that 99 percent of people in the world breathe highly polluted air!

In some places, people wear masks to avoid breathing in poisonous smog.

Poisonous Progress

Industry, which includes factories and construction projects, is another major source of air pollution. Coal-fueled power plants release most of the **particulate matter** that pollutes the air. These are small pieces of dirt, dust, and soot that can make breathing difficult. At its most extreme, particulate matter can even poison a person's bloodstream.

Construction projects produce an outsized percentage of the world's carbon dioxide pollution. This is due, in no small part, to the fact that they rely on fuel-burning **generators** for power.

Some coal-burning power plants release mercury. This extremely dangerous chemical can travel thousands of miles in the air before falling to Earth. As it settles into water and on land, mercury can poison vegetation and wildlife.

Up in Smoke

Where there's fire, there's smoke. And that smoke can be deadly, adding to the pollution in our air. Smoke from fires that burn in forests, on farms, and even at campsites is dangerous to breathe.

Most smoke is a **toxic** mixture of gases, chemicals, and particulate matter. Breathing it in can make a person's throat sore and their eyes water. It can also lead to more serious health problems, including **asthma**, lung **infections**, heart attacks, and strokes.

Trees take in carbon dioxide. When they burn in a wildfire, this carbon is released back into the atmosphere.

Home Is Where the Harm Is

Outdoor smoke, with all its poisonous pollution, can easily seep into peoples' homes. But this is not the only danger inside. Indoor air pollution kills more than 3 million people every year, including more than 500,000 children under the age of 5.

About a third of people worldwide cook with open fires or fuel stoves that pollute the air. Common fuel-burning appliances, such as furnaces and water heaters, are also a problem. They emit poisonous gases and produce their own particulate matter.

> Fresh paint, new furniture, and even carpet can let off the toxic chemicals that were used to make them. Air fresheners, bleaches, detergents, and many cleaning products also release gases that can make people sick.

Emissions from indoor appliances and fires often stay trapped inside.

Fertile Fields
Takachar

In some places in the world, farmers burn their fields after harvest to clear away **stubble** and weeds. But these fires create smoke that leads to harmful air pollution. Thankfully, there are creative minds working to solve this.

A company named Takachar invented a system that clears fields without burning. They make small, inexpensive machines that farmers can drag through their fields to collect crop stubble and weeds. The technology then converts the field waste into **fertilizer** and clean-burning fuel. This system can reduce a farm's smoke emissions by about 98 percent.

Agricultural fires are responsible for about 5 percent of the world's black carbon emissions. This pollutant enters the body through the lungs and bloodstream and can cause long-term health risks.

Takachar founder and CEO, Vidyut Mohan (*pictured*), is an advocate for climate solutions.

Battery Power
Ampd Energy

The construction industry is responsible for more than a third of greenhouse gas emissions worldwide. Much of this pollution is released by the diesel generators that power worksite operations.

To solve this problem, a company called Ampd Energy has created the Enertainer—a large metal box that holds 30,000 rechargeable batteries similar to those found in electric cars. These batteries store energy that can power even the largest construction equipment without burning fossil fuels. Workers can simply plug in and get building!

> The Enertainer has been used for more than 200 construction projects. Its clean power has prevented the release of more than 77,000 tn. (70,000 t) of carbon dioxide.

The Enertainer can provide energy to a variety of high-power equipment, including cranes and welders.

Green Machines
Roam

For many, motorcycles are the easiest and cheapest way to get around. But gasoline-powered motorcycles contribute to global greenhouse gas emissions. So, the company Roam came up with a solution. The Roam Air is an electric motorcycle that can be plugged into any outlet. The Air can travel at more than 55 miles per hour (90 kph) and carry up to 485 lbs. (220 kgs)—all without releasing pollutants.

Roam has also developed a fully electric bus. It can hold 90 passengers, drive up to 43 mph (70 kph), and travel more than 200 miles (320 km) on a single charge.

Each Roam Air comes with two batteries so one can be charging while the other is being used to drive.

Clean Cooking
Mukuru Clean Stove

About 2.3 billion people around the world use open fires and stoves to heat water and cook meals. The resulting indoor air pollution injures or kills millions of people a year.

Innovator Charlot Magayi and her daughter kept getting throat and lung infections from their charcoal-burning stove. After her daughter was severely burned by the stove, Magayi designed a safer, cleaner way to cook—the Mukuru Clean Stove. This stove burns 90 percent cleaner than wood fires and 70 percent cleaner than charcoal stoves. It uses a cheaper fuel made from sugarcane and wood mixed with charcoal.

> More than 415,000 Mukuru Clean Stoves have been sold in Magayi's home country of Kenya. They cost $10 each and have saved more than $50 million in fuel costs.

These stoves are made from recycled waste metal, reducing scrap metal pollution.

Breathing Easier

Almost nothing is more important to life than the air we breathe. Knowing that the air all around us is polluted can seem overwhelming. But luckily, people are working hard on creative solutions to reduce air pollution.

No corner of the world remains unaffected by the air pollution in our atmosphere. We have no choice but to pull together to clean the air for today and into the future. By working together, we can save our Earth and begin to breathe a lot easier.

The Blue Map App gives its users **data** about air and water quality in their area. With this information at their fingertips, people can be empowered to lead healthier lives.

Reduce Air Pollution!

Reducing air pollution can seem like a big job. But even small, everyday steps can help make the air around us a little cleaner. When we each do our part, we can create a large movement with a big impact!

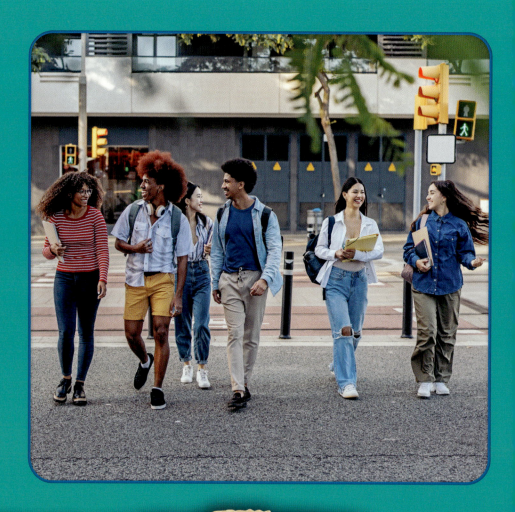

When possible, choose an alternative to taking a fuel-burning car. Walk, bike, or take public transportation to get where you are going.

Encourage your family to consider electric options when buying new household appliances and vehicles.

Limit indoor and outdoor wood fires.

Electricity is often made by burning fossil fuels. Save electricity by turning off lights and unplugging electronics when you're not using them.

Get involved! Join and volunteer for clean air organizations.

Glossary

acid rain a harmful type of rain that contains chemicals called acids; acid rain can be harmful to plants, animals, and buildings

asthma a lung disease that makes it hard to breathe

atmosphere the layer of gases that surrounds Earth

carbon dioxide an invisible gas in the air that is released when fossil fuels are burned

data information and facts, such as measurements

emissions substances, such as gases and soot, released into the air by fuel-burning engines

exhaust smoke and other gases released when fossil fuels burn

fertilizer a substance added to soil to make plants grow better

fossil fuels sources of energy made from the remains of animals and plants that lived long ago

generators machines that use engines to create electricity

infections diseases caused by something harmful entering the body

oxygen a colorless gas found in air and water that people and other animals need to breathe

particulate matter a mixture of tiny pieces of solid and liquid material found in the air, including soot, dust, dirt, and smoke

smog a fog of air pollution

stubble the short growths that remain in a farm field after cutting and harvesting

toxic poisonous and potentially deadly

Read More

Bergin, Raymond. *Fires Everywhere (What on Earth? Climate Change Explained).* Minneapolis: Bearport Publishing, 2022.

Harris, Beatrice. *Jobs in Environmental Science (Inside Guide: STEM Careers).* New York: Cavendish Square, 2024.

Wroble, Susan. *Using Engineering to Fight Climate Change (Fighting Climate Change with Science).* Lake Elmo, MN: Focus Readers, 2023.

Learn More Online

1. Go to **FactSurfer.com** or scan the QR code below.
2. Enter "**Reducing Air Pollution**" into the search box.
3. Click on the cover of this book to see a list of websites.

Index

asthma 14
atmosphere 6–9, 14, 26
carbon dioxide 6, 8, 13–14, 20
chemicals 4, 13–14, 16
construction 9, 12–13, 20
dust 12
emissions 10, 17–18, 20, 22
energy 6, 8, 14, 20
exhaust 4
fires 4, 14, 16–18, 24, 29
fossil fuels 8–9, 20, 29
gasoline 22
infection 14, 24
oxygen 6, 10
particulate matter 12, 14, 16
poison 4, 10–13, 16
smog 4, 10–11
smoke 4, 14, 16, 18
soot 12
stove 16, 24–25
transportation 10, 29

About the Author

Raymond Bergin is a writer living in New Jersey, a state that is often placed under air quality alerts. As someone who has asthma, he takes air pollution and air quality very seriously. He plants lots of trees on his property to help make the local air a little bit cleaner and healthier.